# NOTE TO PARENTS

Although every magic trick in this book has been kid-tested, and can, with practice, be easily performed by most children, some tricks are more difficult than others and may require your supervision. Please read every trick before allowing your child to do it. The RGA Publishing Group and SMITHMARK Publishers will not be held responsible for any injury that occurs during the practice or performance of a trick.

## An RGA Book

# Hoppin' Magic

## My First
## Card & Coin
## MAGIC
## TRICKS

**Written by Stephanie Johnson**

**Illustrated by Kerry Manwaring**

SMITHMARK

# The Vanishing Coin

In an instant, make an ordinary penny disappear!

## What You'll Need:

- A clear glass
- Scissors
- A penny
- A black-and-white section of newspaper
- Rubber cement or glue
- A large handkerchief or cloth

## Getting Ready:

**1.** Put rubber cement or glue around the rim of the glass.

**2.** Turn the glass over and press the rim onto a sheet of newspaper so that it sticks. Let it dry overnight.

**3.** Cut away the extra newspaper around the glass. The mouth of the glass should be covered with a round piece of paper, but no paper should be hanging over the edge.

# Doing the Trick:

**1.** Begin by setting a sheet of newspaper on your show table. Holding the glass so no one can see the round piece of newspaper on it, put the glass upside down on the sheet of newspaper.

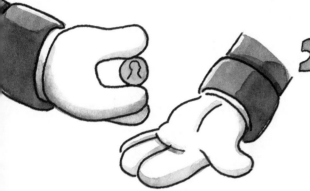

**2.** Ask to borrow a penny from a member of your audience. If no one has a penny, use yours. Hold up the penny and say, "I have here an ordinary penny. I will now make it disappear!"

**3.** Put the penny on the newspaper next to the glass. Lay the handkerchief over the glass and say some magic words.

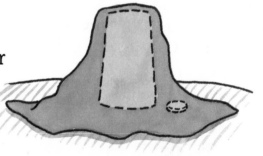

**4.** While the glass is covered with the handkerchief, pick it up and put it on top of the penny. The round piece of newspaper on the glass will hide the penny.

**5.** Remove the handkerchief and say, "Voilà! The penny has vanished!"

# A Penny Lost ...

With a little practice, you'll be able to perform this vanishing trick with ease!

## What You'll Need:
- A penny
- Scissors
- 3 paper (or Styrofoam) cups

## Getting Ready:

1. Cut the rim off one of the cups.

2. Insert one of the two remaining cups into the rimless cup to make a "double cup" that looks like one cup.

## Doing the Trick:

1. Start by setting the double cup and the remaining plain cup on your show table. Say, "Here are two ordinary cups."

2. Hold up the penny and say, "And here is an ordinary penny."

Now say, "I sometimes have a hard time holding onto my money." Drop the penny into the plain cup.

4. Pick up the double cup and slide it inside the plain cup. Tell the audience, "My money just goes and goes."

5. Now separate the double cup by pulling out the rimmed cup and leaving the rimless cup behind, which will cover and hide the penny. Your audience will think there is only one cup remaining when there are really two.

6. Pick up the new double cup and show the inside to your audience. The penny is gone!

# ... **I**s a **P**enny **F**ound

MAGIC, MAGIC, FAR AND NEAR,
MAKE A PENNY NOW APPEAR!

After you have dazzled your audience with the previous trick, try this one on them!

## **W**hat **Y**ou'll **N**eed:

Use the same objects you used in **A Penny Lost** . . .

## **G**etting **R**eady:

1. Put the penny into the rimless cup.

2. Slide a rimmed cup into the rimless cup to cover the penny and create a "double cup" that looks like one cup

## **D**oing the **T**rick:

1. Put the double cup and the plain cup on your table. Show the audience that both cups are empty.

**2.** Say, "I have an easy time making money. I don't have to work. The pennies just come to me." Pick up the double cup and slide it inside the plain cup.

**3.** Wave your wand over the cups and say, "Magic, magic, far and near, make a penny now appear!"

**4.** Separate the double cup by lifting the rimmed cup out. The rimless cup remains inside the plain cup to create a new double cup.

**5.** Pick up the double cup and tip it over. Out comes the penny!

# Trading Places

Make two coins mysteriously switch places with just a few magic words!

## What You'll Need:

- ▲ 2 pennies
- ▲ A nickel
- ▲ 2 medium-sized paper bags

## Getting Ready:

1. Roll down the edges of both paper bags so that you can look inside them easily.

2. Practice hiding a penny in the palm of your hand as shown. You may want to stick a piece of tape to the back of the penny as you practice.

## Doing the Trick:

1. Hide one penny in the palm of your hand, and set the other penny and the nickel on your show table.

2. Put the bags on the table, one at each end. Then say, "I have here a penny and a nickel, and two magic paper bags."

3. Hold up the bags and show that they are empty. *Be careful not to let anyone see the penny hidden in your hand.*

Now pick up the nickel, using the fingers of the hand in which you are holding the penny. Say, "Watch carefully as I put the nickel into one bag."

5. Put your hand in one bag. Pretend to drop the nickel into the bag, *but drop the hidden penny into the bag instead.* Hide the nickel in your palm and take your hand out of the bag.

6. With the same hand, pick up the penny from the show table with your fingers. Say, "Now I'm going to put the penny in the other bag."

7. Put your hand in the other bag, *but instead of dropping the penny, drop the nickel into the bag.* Before pulling your hand out of the bag, hide the penny in your palm. Then secretly drop the penny into your pocket.

8. Now wave your magic wand over the bags and say, "Magic wand, make the coins magically switch places!"

9. Ask the audience, "Which bag did I drop the nickel into?" When they answer, ask for a volunteer to come up and pull out the coin inside each bag. The nickel and penny will have traded places!

# Double Your Money!

ALAKAZAM, ALAKAFUNS,
WHERE THERE WERE NONE,
NOW THERE ARE TONS !!

Here's a trick that will show you how to "make" money!

## What You'll Need:

★ 2 pennies
★ An empty matchbox (the kind with a sliding drawer)

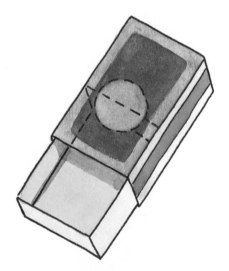

## Getting Ready:

**1.** Open the matchbox drawer halfway.

**2.** Wedge one penny between the back edge of the drawer and the top of the box. Put the other penny in your pock

## Doing the Trick:

**1.** Show the half-opened matchbox to your audience. Let a volunteer look inside to see that the drawer is empty. Don't let him or her hold the matchbox, though!

2. Ask, "Does anyone have a penny I could borrow?" Use this penny as the second penny during the trick. If no one happens to have a penny, use the one in your pocket.

3. Say, "This is a magic matchbox that doubles your money. Watch carefully as I put this penny into the drawer."

4. Put the penny into the matchbox. Show the box to someone in the audience so he or she can see that there is only one penny in the drawer. Again, don't let anyone hold the box!

5. Close the matchbox drawer. When you do so, the wedged penny will drop down into the drawer.

6. Wave your wand over the matchbox and say, "Alakazam, alakazoo! Where there was one, now there are two!" Open the drawer and proudly show the two pennies inside!

# The Missing Penny

Fool your audience into seeing double with this mind-boggling trick!

## What You'll Need:

- ◆ A small paper bag
- ◆ A penny
- ◇ 2 identical playing cards

## Getting Ready:

1. Place one playing card flat on the bottom of the paper bag and crunch the top of the bag together.

## Doing the Trick:

1. Put the paper bag, the other playing card, and the penny on your show table. Say to your audience, "I have here an ordinary paper bag, a simple playing card, and a penny."

2. Pick up the bag in one hand and say, "Now watch very carefully."

**3.** Pick up the card with your other hand and put it into the bag. Then pick up the penny and put it into the bag too.

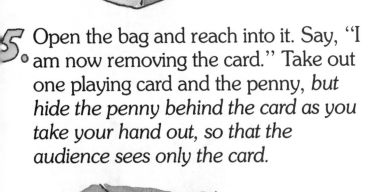

**4.** Squeeze the bag closed at the top and shake it. Put it down on the table and wave your magic wand over it.

**5.** Open the bag and reach into it. Say, "I am now removing the card." Take out one playing card and the penny, *but hide the penny behind the card as you take your hand out, so that the audience sees only the card.*

**6.** Drop the card and the penny into your pocket.

**7.** Ask the audience, "What do you think is still in the bag?" They will say, "the penny." Have a volunteer come up and pull out what is inside the bag. It will be the other playing card!

# The Soft Coin

Cut a quarter into quarters with this mind-boggling trick!

## What You'll Need:

- ✄ A quarter  ✄ Scissors
- ✄ A piece of heavy paper, 6 inches by 6 inches

## Getting Ready:

There is not much preparation needed for this trick, but you must practice it several times before you perform it.

## Doing the Trick:

1. Show the paper and the quarter to your audience and say, "I have here an ordinary quarter and an ordinary piece of paper."

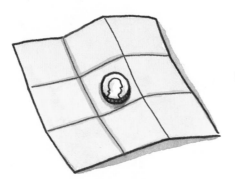

2. Fold the paper into thirds vertically. Then unfold the paper and fold it into thirds horizontally. When you unfold it again, you should have nine squares.

3. Put the quarter on the middle square.

4. Fold the side flaps over the quarter one at a time to cover it. Fold the top flap down.

**5.** Before you fold up the bottom flap, lift up the paper slightly and tip it toward you, letting the quarter slip down into the bottom flap. Don't let the audience see this! Then fold up the bottom flap.

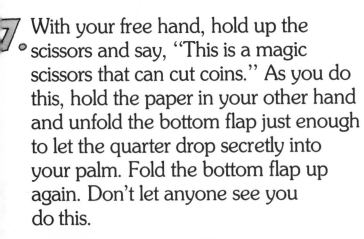

**6.** Now rub the paper around the edge of the quarter to make a coin-shaped crease in the paper. Ask a volunteer to come onstage and feel the paper to make sure the coin is still there. *Do not let the volunteer hold the paper, because the coin might fall out.*

**7.** With your free hand, hold up the scissors and say, "This is a magic scissors that can cut coins." As you do this, hold the paper in your other hand and unfold the bottom flap just enough to let the quarter drop secretly into your palm. Fold the bottom flap up again. Don't let anyone see you do this.

**8.** Say, "I will now show you I can cut quarters." Cut the paper crosswise into four pieces.

**9.** Put down the scissors and throw the pieces of paper into the air. The quarter has vanished!

# Spooky Cards

You can make playing cards magically stick to your hand—without using glue or paste!

## What You'll Need:

- Playing cards
- A ring
- A toothpick

## Getting Ready:

**1.** Put on the ring.

**2.** Turn your hand palm side up. Slide the toothpick under the ring.

## Doing the Trick:

**1.** Place your hand, palm side down, on your show table. *Be careful not to let the audience see the toothpick.* Say, "I will now slip several playing cards under my hand and then magically lift them all at once without grabbing onto them."

**2.** With your free hand, take a playing card and slide it under the hand that is on the table. Make sure to also slide the card under one end of the toothpick.

**3.** Take another card and slide it under your hand, putting it between your hand and the other end of the toothpick.

**4.** Once these two cards are securely in place, they will hold the other cards. Slide about 6 more cards under your hand.

**5.** Say, "Abracadabra!" and slowly lift your hand from the table. The cards will stick to the palm of your hand!

# Find the Card

THIS TRICK IS GREAT, IT'S NOT SO HARD... I BET I'LL PICK THE MAGIC CARD!

Baffle your friends with your special deck of cards!

## What You'll Need:

☐ A deck of "one way" marked cards*
■ Fine-line markers, red and black

## Getting Ready:

1. Go through your deck of cards and make sure all the marks you've made are at the top.

*How to make "one way" marked cards: Take an ordinary deck of playing cards and put them face up. Using a fine-line marker, make a tiny dot on each card in the upper left-hand corner. If the suit is red, use a red marker. If the suit is black, use a black marker. Before you use these cards in the trick, make sure all the markings are in the upper left-hand corner. You will be able to see the markings, but your audience will not.

# Doing the Trick:

**1.** Fan out the cards and let someone from the audience pick a card. Tell the person to look at it and memorize it.

**2.** While the volunteer is looking at the card, secretly turn the deck around in your hand and fan them out again.

**3.** Ask the volunteer to return the chosen card to the deck. Make sure its marking is facing the opposite way from the rest of the deck. Shuffle the cards, but be careful to keep the cards facing in the same direction.

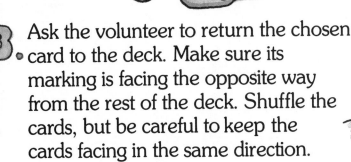

**4.** Have the volunteer cut the cards. Wave your wand over the cards and say, "Magic wand, it's not so hard, help me find the chosen card!"

**5.** Pick up the deck and fan through it until you find the one that is turned around.

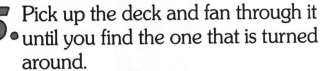

**6.** Hold up the card and ask, "Is this the card you picked?" It will be!

# Easy Penny

SHAZOO, SHAZAM, SHALENNIES, THESE COINS ARE EASY PENNIES !!

You'll be "in the money" with this astounding trick!

## What You'll Need:

☆ A small paper bag
★ Putty or chewed chewing gum
★ 10 to 15 pennies
★ A pencil

## Getting Ready:

1. Put the pennies into the bag.

2. Put a small amount of chewing gum o putty under your fingernail.

## Doing the Trick:

1. Start by asking for a volunteer from your audience. Give him or her the pencil. Have your volunteer take a penny from the bag and read the date on the penny out loud. Ask him or her to make a pencil mark on the penny. Hold out your hand and tell the volunteer to give the penny to you.

**2.** Close your fingers around the penny. Quickly rub some of the gum or putty onto it, pressing the gum or putty to make it stick. Don't let the audience see you do this.

**3.** With your free hand, wave your magic wand over the penny and say, "Shazoo shazam shalenny! Make this an Easy Penny!"

**4.** Now drop the penny into the bag with the other pennies. Shake the bag to mix them up.

**5.** Wave your wand over the bag and say, "Easy Penny, show yourself!"

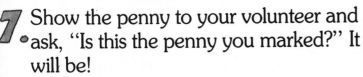

**6.** Reach into the bag and find the penny with the gum or putty stuck to it. As you take the penny out of the bag, quickly scrape off the sticky stuff.

**7.** Show the penny to your volunteer and ask, "Is this the penny you marked?" It will be!

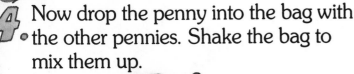

# Into Thin Air

## What You'll Need:

- A toothpick
- A deck of cards
- A handkerchief with a hem
- Scissors

## Getting Ready:

**1.** Cut the toothpick so that it is as long as the width of the playing card.

**2.** Poke the cut toothpick into the hem of the handkerchief.

## Doing the Trick:

**1.** Begin by spreading the deck of cards on your show table. Hold up the handkerchief. Tell your audience, "I will now pick up a card from this deck and make it vanish into thin air!"

**2.** Lay the handkerchief over the cards so that the edge with the toothpick is bent underneath the handkerchief.

**3.** Pick up the edge of the handkerchief that contains the toothpick. Hold it between your thumb and forefinger. It will look as though you have picked up one of the cards.

**4.** Say, "Alakazam, alakazeer, make this playing card disappear!" Throw the handkerchief up into the air. The card will seem to have vanished!

# Merlin's Box

In this trick, one dime seems to jump magically from one box to another!

## What You'll Need:

- ☐ A thin, stiff piece of cardboard (2½ inches wide and 6 inches long)
- ☐ A small balloon
- ☐ 2 identical empty matchboxes (the kind with the sliding drawer)
- ☐ 4 small rubber bands
- ☐ 2 dimes
- ☐ A large safety pin
- ☐ A pencil, ruler, and tape

## Getting Ready:

**1.** With the ruler, mark off 1 inch, then ¼ inch, then 1 inch, then another ¼ inch across each short end of the cardboard. Then use the ruler and pencil to connect the marks on each end.

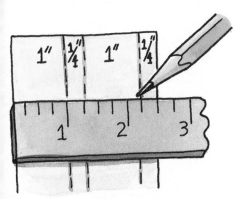

**2.** Fold the cardboard along the lines you drew and tape it together as shown. This will be your "coin slide."

**3.** Insert one end of the coin slide into the opening of the balloon.

**4.** Slide open the drawer of one matchbox. Put the balloon inside the drawer and slide the drawer closed as far as it will go. The coin slide will stick out of the drawer.

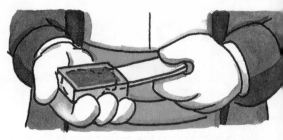

**5.** Put two rubber bands around the matchbox to hold the drawer closed.

**6.** Put the safety pin through just one side of the coin slide and pin it to the inside of your jacket.

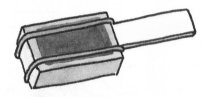

**7.** Put the dimes, the remaining rubber bands, and the other matchbox in your pocket. Practice this trick several times before performing it!

## Doing the Trick:

**1.** Hide one dime in the palm of your hand. Hold up the other dime and ask a volunteer to put a pencil mark on the dime.

**2.** Say, "I'm going to put this dime into a matchbox and seal it well, because these coins like to jump from box to box." Take the empty matchbox from your pocket. Pretend to put the marked dime into it, *but instead drop in the dime that is hidden in your hand.* Hide the marked dime in your palm.

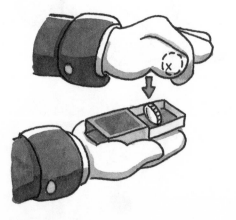

**3.** Put the remaining two rubber bands around the matchbox to keep it shut. Give the box to the volunteer.

**4.** Say, "I have an identical matchbox inside my jacket." Reach into your jacket to fetch the box. Quickly put the marked coin into the coin slide. It will slip into the balloon.

**5.** Carefully slide the box off the coin slide. When you do, the rubber bands will force the drawer completely shut.

**6.** Show the audience the matchbox from your jacket. Ask the volunteer to open the matchbox he or she is holding. The volunteer will find a dime with no pencil mark.

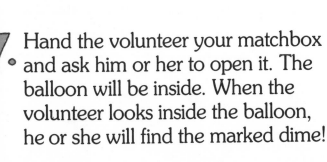

**7.** Hand the volunteer your matchbox and ask him or her to open it. The balloon will be inside. When the volunteer looks inside the balloon, he or she will find the marked dime!